Best of Luck!

Tony Fadoor

6/25/2009

Tony Fadool

The Grass Is Always
Greener
When You Water It

Common Sense Ways To Grow Your Sales

Printed in the United States of America
First printing 2005
ISBN 0-9770208-0-0

Editorial supervision by Cynthia Tomczak
Creative concept by Julie Long and Patricia Tsagaris
Book design by Patricia Tsagaris
Photographs on pages 13, 21, 63 and 79 by Ric Evans

To my beautiful wife, Winnie, for your love, inspiration, patience and great sense of humor.

To my kids, Perry, Elizabeth, Lewis, Michael, and Amy, the smartest and funniest young people I know. Thanks for your love. I continue to learn more from each of you than you can imagine.

To my late parents for the sacrifices and guidance that have made me who I am.

And to the many great salespeople I have worked with, or who have worked for me. Each of you has been a special gift in my life.

Acknowledgements

I want to thank Julie Long for her hard work, her attention to detail, and her considerable writing skills in helping me put this collection of thoughts and ideas into a readable book. You are a gifted writer and a very patient person. Thanks to Patricia Tsagaris for her terrific creative design and visual expertise.

Thanks to all of my good friends in Federated's Marketing and Corporate Communications department for their hard work and ideas. Thank you to Gene and Judy Maloney for your friendship, for the many great moments of inspiration, Gene's dry sense of humor, and the use of your fantastic yard for the book jacket. Special thanks to Cynthia Tomczak, who kept everyone on schedule and literally brought all the pieces together. And I especially thank my company, Federated Investors, for their enthusiastic support. A company of friends is good company indeed.

Investment sales is a rather strange business compared to most. We sell a product no one can see yet everyone can describe. We have a service that is vital to a person's long-term financial health, yet few people want to talk to us about it. Worst of all, we tend to get the blame when the market is down, and when the market is up, instead of appreciating our efforts our customers think they can do it themselves. On the face of it, this doesn't sound like a very appealing environment for a salesperson.

But those of us who have been in the business through several decades and market cycles know that selling investments can be quite rewarding — not only financially, but also in terms of helping people. Few careers can bring as much satisfaction as attending the college graduation of the child of a good customer and knowing you were instrumental in helping accumulate the savings to pay for it. Or watching a client begin a dream retirement after you helped grow her nest egg over the past 20 years.

Sales as a career path is so much larger than just making the sale. I've watched a lot of men and women burn out after spending 10 or 15 years in sales regardless of the success they've achieved. In studying this phenomenon I've determined that what "burned out" was not their ability to perform, but rather their enjoyment of the process itself.

I remember a terrific salesperson who worked for me for several years and won nearly every sales award we had to offer. One day he came to me and said he was quitting sales. When I asked why, he replied that he just didn't want the pressure of trying to hit goals every month and was looking to get into a less stressful environment.

I invited him to lunch and we talked for quite a while. He came to realize that the stress he was feeling wasn't because of numbers or quotas, it was because he had no vision of what his career was all about. He had gotten to the point where winning the awards and getting the recognition wasn't motivating him any longer. He needed to change his perception of why he does what he does.

I helped him see that selling isn't about the sales awards and recognition. You can only sustain passion for a sales goal for the quarter, or maybe the year. Beyond that sort of goal, you need a higher purpose to what you are doing. Ultimately, for all of us, it can't be about what *we* achieve but rather about what we help *others* achieve.

When that salesman began to see the wonderful things he had done for his customers, the great relationships he had developed and the need that those customers — and future customers — had for his knowledge and advice, then the spark of passion was reignited in him. And it has stayed with him for 20 more years. He gets up early and looks forward to another day of helping someone fulfill a dream or solve a problem, or perhaps just making their day go a little easier. He is looked up to by his peers and respected by his competitors. But most importantly, he is loved by his customers.

This is how I hope you will look at your career in sales. This book isn't about winning the sales awards (although it will help you do so) and it isn't just about ideas to help you close more business (although you will). This book is about changing your perspective on why you are here and what role you can play in the lives of your customers. I hope to give you a new definition of success and to shape your thinking and your sales approach toward a much higher purpose. In nearly 40 years of sales, I've been through the gamut of market environments and customer situations. I couldn't help but learn a few things (most of them the hard way). If my perspective can help other salespeople as they face similar situations — if I can help you avoid some of the pitfalls and capitalize on more opportunities — then I will have served my purpose in writing this book and achieved my definition of success.

CONTENTS

PART ONE

Laying the Groundwork

CHAPTER ONE

The grass is always greener when you water it

Cultivate Your Own Greener Pastures

"Do not despise or hate your neighbor because he has been a success;
take care of your own case."

—WILLIAM TECUMSEH VERNON

We've all been there. Someone else's career looks better. Their client list is stronger, their product much easier to sell, their company so much more supportive. At least it looks that way from your side of the fence.

You can have what the other guy has — heck, you can have *more* than the other guy. In fact, it's right under your feet: Your own plot of potential. It can become the greener pasture you're looking for, *if you just water it.*

The only way to succeed in sales is to work at it. Few sales professionals are willing to accept this fact — even fewer are willing to put forth the effort. Instead they complain about their circumstances, begrudge their competitors' successes, and rationalize their own failures with "if only." If only they'd put that much effort into improving themselves and their approach to sales!

This book will cover more than a dozen common sense approaches to grow your sales, but at the heart of all of them are three prerequisites to success. I call them the AAAs. If you aren't willing to accept them as fundamental truths, you might as well close this book now.

THE FIRST A: ACCOUNTABILITY

You are 100% responsible for your life

"Ninety-nine percent of all failures come from people who have a habit of making excuses."

—GEORGE WASHINGTON CARVER

Take responsibility for everything that occurs in your life, both the successes and the failures. If your grass isn't green, it's because you've chosen not to water it.

If you're reading this book, you have an image — perhaps just a glimpse — of something better. How will you find the way to make that vision a reality?

The answer isn't by looking at what you could have, would make, should get. You'll only find it when you look inside to what you can be, can do, can change. Business philosopher Jim Rohn reminds us that we cannot change circumstances; we can only change ourselves.

Psychologists cite this simple formula for taking responsibility:

$$E + R = O$$
Event + Response = Outcome

Everything you've experienced in life is the result of how you have responded to an earlier event. If you don't like the outcomes you are currently getting, you have two choices: You can blame the event, which basically means complaining about something. Or you can change your responses to the way things are — change what you think, do and communicate — until you get the outcome you want.

My colleague Ray and I were invited to golf as the guests of some very important prospects. We were nervous on a couple of levels: there was a lot of business at stake, of course, plus we were golfing at Oakmont Country Club, frequent home to the U.S. Open golf tournament.

When Ray went to tee off on the first hole, it was obvious to me he was having trouble focusing; he took several practice swings, then stood over the ball fidgeting a great deal. Finally he swung his club back with great force and brought it down to whack the ball — and missed! I mean he completely missed the ball, didn't even knock it off the tee. My heart still jumps in my throat just remembering. The member of the club covered his eyes with his hands. The caddies groaned.

Given a similar circumstance, what would you do? How would you respond to an embarrassing event? Would you curse your stupidity? Blame it on your new club?

I'll tell you what my colleague did: He turned to the rest of the foursome, wiped his forehead and said with deadpan seriousness, "Boy, is this a tough course or what?"

That humorous response had the power to turn a negative event into a positive outcome. He endeared himself to the prospects and we landed the account.

THE SECOND A: ATTITUDE

Whether you think you can or think you can't, you're right

"Whatever the mind can conceive and believe, it can achieve."

—NAPOLEON HILL

I once heard a story about an old chief talking to a young brave over a campfire. The young boy asked the chief, "What is a pessimist and what is an optimist?"

The chief replied that the boy should think of them as two dogs within every person. "The optimist is a bright dog that sees good in everything. The pessimist is a dark dog that only sees the bad in everything. The two dogs are always fighting each other."

"Which dog wins?" asked the young brave.

The chief replied, "The one you feed the most."

Which dog are you feeding the most?

The Power of Positive Thinking

Brain researchers have discovered that with a positive attitude combined with training, coaching and practice, anyone can learn to do almost anything. Isn't that amazing?

But you've got to believe you can do it. You've got to expect it will happen — because you get what you expect.

You've no doubt heard of positive visualization, especially in the arena of professional and Olympic athletes. It's the act of picturing yourself achieving a goal.

Positive visualization works because the brain cannot differentiate between an experience that is envisioned and one that actually happens. Whether it's an actual memory or a make-believe scene, it's all filed in the same place. Based on a lifetime of these experiences — real or envisioned — the brain is conditioned to expect what comes next. And because our brain expects something to happen in a certain way, we often achieve what we anticipate.

The key to visualization is that the mind must visualize something happening; it cannot visualize something *not* happening. When you tell yourself not to be nervous when presenting to a big prospect, there is no image of "not" — in fact, you're likely to picture yourself being nervous. However, when you think of smiling with confidence while your prospect is nodding in agreement, your mind can easily picture that event. Always define and then picture the positive result you are seeking.

Shrug Off Negativity

I read a great book recently called *Zen Golf*, by Dr. Joseph Parent. Dr. Parent has a terrific way of nullifying the negative effect of the bad shot. He says you should never say things like, "I just can't hit a 5 iron," or "I always slice the ball!" Such statements not only increase the negative feelings you have about the shot but also reinforce your conviction that you cannot hit the 5 iron. Instead, when you land in the sand, simply say this: "Hmm, that was interesting." It's neither good, nor bad, just interesting. It takes the negative out of the situation and allows you to react to, but not reinforce, the poor shot. Another expression he suggests: "How unlike me." This creates a positive reinforcement that this sort of mishap is not the norm, but rather the exception, to your usual game.

The next time you fail to close a sale or meet a customer's

expectations, stop yourself from saying things like, "I just can't close a sale this week!" or "These customers just don't understand my product!" You will reinforce this belief in your mind and it will make that next sales call all the more difficult for you. Instead, try using one of Dr. Parent's responses to the event.

Refuse to Have a Bad Day

When you say you're having a bad day, you're really saying you let others affect your attitude. The day isn't bad until you say it's bad. So don't say it. It sounds simple, but it works. Try it, you'll see.

When I'm asked how my day is going, I always say, "Unbelievable!" It can mean many things, but mostly it provides a neutral reaction — not good, not bad — and I can always say it with enthusiasm.

I know a successful insurance broker who never utters the word "bad" when you ask him how his day is. Once in a while he'll use the word "challenging." Isn't that great? He knows challenges are good; they bring forth opportunity.

THE THIRD A: ACTION

You can't spell satisfaction without it

> "If you want to have what you have not,
> you must do what you do not."
>
> —TARO GOLD

Think about the ways salespeople often fall short: not making new contacts, not preparing for an appointment, not asking for a referral. In short, not taking action. Between inaction and action, choose action every time.

Sure, sometimes an action is the wrong action. Yes, you'll make mistakes. But failure is a great teacher — you'll learn what not to do and you most likely won't have to repeat that class again. Recognize that failure carries its own reward. You just have to look for it.

According to a specialist at the University of Notre Dame, 94% of salespeople quit trying by the fourth call — in fact, most quit after the first call. But 60% of all sales are made after the fourth call. When you don't keep trying you're neglecting more than half of your potential sales!

Anticipate rejections and put them into the context of the law of averages. If I close one out of five prospects, then I know that four will not close. Every "no" I encounter just puts me one step closer to the "yes" that I know will eventually occur.

Don't Just Work Harder, Work Smarter

Your priority as a salesperson is to sell, correct? But it's estimated that as much as 80% of the salesperson's time is taken up by activities that don't directly generate business. Don't believe me? Try this exercise: Keep a log of how you spend your time for one week. Chances are your average day will look something like this:

• Internal meetings	20%
• Meeting with other professionals	20%
• Completing reports	10%
• Staying up to date via reading, etc.	5%
• Taking orders (passive)	20%
• Client servicing	15%
• Selling (active) current clients	5%
• Prospecting	<u>5%</u>
	100%

That amounts to only 10% of the time actively selling and prospecting. If you work an eight-hour day, that's only about 48 minutes per day.

Imagine the return you would experience by doubling your selling and prospecting effort. All you need to do is devote an extra 45 minutes or so a day to selling.

Block out 1-1/2 to 2 hours each day for nothing else but selling or prospecting. No meetings, no e-mails, no disruptions — just selling. Put this selling and prospecting time in your appointment book or calendar. Make it a standing appointment that cannot be moved. No exceptions.

Why so strict? Think of it this way: Every meeting that goes long and cuts into your prospecting time could mean a missed opportunity to find that one new high net worth client.

Choose What to Do

So often we adopt a faulty approach of wanting to clear the small stuff off our pile first so we can really focus on the important things. Face this fact: Your "in" basket will never be empty. You must decide how you want to spend your time and energy. Management consultant and coach David Allen puts it simply: "You have more to do than you can possibly do. You just need to feel good about your choices. And you can't feel good about your choices unless you are clear about what your work really is."

An advertising professional I know has completely grasped this principle. Advertising professionals are known for working late nights; there's always an impossible deadline to meet. But now that my friend has adopted a child, she is no longer able to work late nights. And yet her job responsibilities haven't changed. She still has just as much to do in a day — with fewer hours to do it. I asked her how she manages to pull this off. She said every day she goes into work having identified exactly what she must accomplish that day and she focuses on that task, guarding her time ferociously. She doesn't answer personal emails at work, doesn't chitchat by the water cooler, keeps lunch to a half hour, doesn't take on tasks that someone else could handle more efficiently, and says "no" to meetings that could be handled by memo. She is clear about what her work really is. And she chooses that job above all the other "stuff."

Do you have the discipline and courage to say "no" when confronted with distractions and time-wasting activities? Remember, you drive the productivity of your day — and, ultimately, the level of your success.

"Attitude drives actions. Actions drive results. Results drive lifestyles."

—JIM ROHN

CHAPTER TWO

You can't bend over backwards if you don't have a leg to stand on

Be a Person of Integrity

"The truth of the matter is, you always know the right thing to do.
The hard part is doing it."

—General Norman Schwarzkopf

When you operate with honesty, integrity and ethics, you are guaranteed a good return on your investment throughout your career. You may not notice it immediately but, just like we tell our investment clients, you're in the market for the long term.

Integrity has other, short-term pay-offs as well. Operating with integrity means never having to feel guilty. You haven't overstated the benefits or the need to buy. You haven't understated your fees or the risk involved. There's no guilt and nothing to fear, because you have nothing to hide.

What exactly does it mean to have integrity in business? It boils down to three things:

1. Always Put the Interest of the Client before Your Own

Whenever we have a situation in which we are faced with making a choice between our own interests and those of the customer, the solution is always to err on the side of the client. If he wants a stock you know isn't the right vehicle for his needs, forego the commission and tell him. You may lose the sale, but you'll be a better advisor.

Whenever you find yourself rationalizing a sale, let that serve as an indicator that you might have a problem. Many investment advisors rationalized the losses clients incurred from the tech stocks market bubble in the late 1990s and early 2000 by saying, "I just did what the client wanted." But that logic reduced their relationship with the client to that of an order-taker. Did they really believe that was the extent of their role? Or were they simply excusing their own behavior in not assuming accountability for the client's financial well-being, in not voicing their professional opinion even though it might have cost them the sale?

The good sale is a good sale under any scrutiny. If you see it from the perspective of the customer and it passes muster, it's the right decision. If you talk a client into something that's not a good fit, he won't be happy in the long term, you'll have to carry the guilt, and the client will probably end up leaving anyway. Nobody really wins.

2. Always Do What You Say You Will

Whether you make a serious promise or a casual comment, your customers take both as gospel. Take care when you say what you will do; you are giving your word — make sure you can follow through. Even the tiniest matters can become deal-breakers in the future should a problem arise in the relationship.

When it comes to saying "yes," check your calendar, check your workload, *check your true intentions.* Bending over backwards promising this and that means nothing if you can't follow through. If all you can do is look into the matter further, then say so. Then do it and get back to them, even if it's with bad news. Your clients will think better of you when they see that even though you may not commit to everything they want, what you do commit to you darn well deliver.

Keeping promises (and everything is a promise even when you don't state it as such) is essential to maintaining your integrity. And maintaining your integrity earns trust — and referrals.

3. Maintain Your Own Standards of Behavior

You may never have stopped to catalog your standards of behavior, but you know what they are. Stop and think about them now. I can't speak for you, but I can suggest a few:

- *Tell the truth.* Don't be afraid to say you don't know. Your credibility is enhanced when you say, "I'm not certain about that but I will check and get you an answer."
- *Be thankful for their business and show it.* Show it in how you treat them when you interact, as well as the efforts you make when you are not face to face.
- *Do the right thing.* Uphold your fiduciary responsibility. Be able to honestly say, "This is the very best action for my customer."

- ***Don't ever let fear or greed drive your actions.*** Both can be cruel masters. They foster short-term decisions, which are usually bad for long-term careers.
- ***Treat clients with respect.*** Listen to their opinions, concerns and ideas. Try to better understand them rather than dismiss them. By showing genuine interest, you will build a stronger relationship over time.
- ***Don't badmouth any client or competitor.*** When you negate the competitor you negate the customer who made the choice to be with them. Rather than trying to promote yourself as superior, focus on the points of difference between you and a competitor.

Guard your integrity with ferocity. It isn't everything — it is the only thing. People deal with you not for products, but for the peace of mind that comes with working with a trustworthy professional. If you lose that trust and confidence, you have little to offer. Products can be acquired from anyone and any outlet, including the Internet. The customer can, in fact, invest for a lot less cost themselves. Why would they remain loyal to you if not for trust and confidence? Your reputation is your greatest asset.

A man's reputation is like a lighted match. Once extinguished, it is impossible to rekindle.

> "If you don't have integrity in your bones,
> you shouldn't be allowed out on the field."
>
> —JACK WELCH

PART TWO

BUILDING RELATIONSHIPS

CHAPTER THREE

Be willing to give the shirt off your back and offer to tailor it

Don't Focus on Your Product — Focus on Your Clients

"I don't know what your destiny will be, but one thing I know, the only ones among you who will be really happy are those who have sought and found how to serve."

—ALBERT SCHWEITZER

If you desire to have a successful long-term sales career, you must start focusing on what you *give* rather than what you *get*. That means looking beyond the potential business in front of you to the *person* in front of you. Your customers are people — people with fears and hopes, needs and aspirations. Your job is to help them *in any way you can*. Not just with your product. Not only through your service. But by being *of service*.

Being of service is not an obligation. It's an opportunity. Remember the sales credo Zig Ziglar always preached: "You can have everything in life you want if you will just help enough other people get what they want."

The way to become successful is to first make other people successful. Put your clients' needs first. Always ask how you can help. Always be thinking about what you can do for them.

GIVE WITHOUT EXPECTATION

It's a mystery of life that if you do something expecting praise and recognition, it will seldom come. But when recognition isn't the end result you seek — when you do something simply because it's the right thing — recognition very often comes to you anyway.

If you give without expectation, I promise, eventually the benefits will come back to you. Whatever value you give, it will flow back to you tenfold.

SHARE YOUR RESOURCES

In his *New York Times* bestseller *Love is the Killer App*, Tim Sanders discusses the importance of "sharing your intangibles" to achieve professional success. There are three types of intangibles you should share:

1. *Your Knowledge* — everything you have acquired through observation, experience, conversation and books
2. *Your Network* — everyone you know, because each is a potential partner for every person you meet
3. *Your Compassion* — the ability to reach out with warmth, be it eye contact, physical touch or words

Sanders makes the case that people who share generously are able, among other things, to build a strong personal brand (which is key to setting yourself apart from the competition), create an experience (which is superseding service as the economic focus), and access people's attention rather than just their time (which speaks to a higher level of commitment to you).

In a world of proprietary information and trade secrets, the word "sharing" can illicit gasps of alarm comparable to hearing the words "information leak" or "corporate mole." But sharing — the simple principle we all learned in kindergarten — may be the missing link in many a salesperson's approach. Let's consider more closely the power of sharing your resources with your clients:

- *Sharing strengthens your bond.* When you share something with your clients — a great book, a personal experience or an interesting story — you extend the number of conversation topics you can share.
- *Sharing keeps you connected.* When you introduce a client to a person or some useful piece of information, you naturally have a reason to follow up and reconnect.
- *Sharing increases your worth.* When clients can turn to you for so much more than products and services, you become more important to them.
- *Sharing makes you irreplaceable.* Clients come to rely on your knowledge, network and compassion. What you offer, they could never find with anyone else.

Remember what we learned when we were five: It's nice to share. It's also a smart business practice.

VALUE RELATIONSHIPS OVER RESULTS

A study conducted by Investor's Research, Inc. showed that, when it comes to investment advisors, the top six priorities for clients were all relational in nature:

1. *Understand my situation*
2. *Educate me*
3. *Respect my assets (no matter how small)*
4. *Solve my problem — don't sell me a product*
5. *Monitor my progress*
6. *Keep in touch*

It's obvious that clients value relationships over results. You should too. When you do the opposite — when you value results over relationships and go directly for the outcome — you make others feel used. You devalue them. Recognize that the means are an important part of the end.

RAISE THE BAR

What is your purpose as a salesperson? To sell a quality product that customers need? To provide a valuable service? Why not reach a little higher?

Try using a "purpose hierarchy." This is a tool outlined in the book *Breakthrough Thinking: The Seven Principles of Creative Problem Solving*, by Gerald Nadler and Shozo Hibino.

The objective of a purpose hierarchy is to expand your thinking about a problem, challenge or opportunity. Start by stating the most basic purpose of something. Then ask yourself, "What's the purpose of that?" When you have an answer, ask yourself the question again. Keep going until you work your way up to the largest purpose you can imagine.

An investment professional might consider the most basic purpose of his job to be selling investments and financial advice.

But what is the purpose of that?
To help clients achieve their financial goals.

But what is the purpose of that?
To enable clients to pursue their dreams.

But what is the purpose of that?
To bring fulfillment and joy to clients' lives.

When you focus on serving your clients with that higher purpose, what you will become is more than a salesperson, even more than a trusted advisor. *You will become a purely positive force in your clients' lives.*

Working at this higher purpose, you'll find that your actions naturally go beyond products and services to include anything and everything that brings joy and fulfillment. Sure, it includes designing a financial portfolio that provides your clients with financial independence. But it might also include researching a surfing school for a client because you know he has always wanted to learn.

Once I happened to mention to my insurance agent that when I golfed my greatest difficulty was getting out of the sand bunker. Weeks later I was opening my mail and was delighted to find he'd sent me an article he'd come across with tips on hitting out of sand traps. I was touched he'd even remembered my problem and flattered he took the time to send the article.

A friend of mine was talking to one of his clients about fishing. The client mentioned how much his dad loved to fish and that it had been years since they'd gone fishing together. He had fond childhood memories of that time spent together; it was a tradition he intended to start with his own five-year-old son. That summer my friend invited his client to come fish in a pond on his property and to bring his dad and son. A few weeks later he sent his client a photo he had taken of the three generations of fishermen. The client called to thank him, clearly touched by his kindness, and shared how his father and son hadn't stopped talking about the day. My friend and his client agreed to make it an annual event.

When you are providing that level of enhancement to a person's joy, it earns you a permanent spot in their life. It also gives you a true feeling of warmth.

At the end of the day, it isn't about assets under management, fees generated or our performance relative to a benchmark. It is about only one thing: people, and our willingness to help them.

> "When you are able to help others grow to become
> the best people they can be... you, too, grow."
>
> —MILTON MAYEROFF

CHAPTER FOUR

What's good for the goose, the gander might not like

Adjust Your Communication Style to Suit Your Client

"I've been told that I talk in shorthand and then smudge it."
—J.R.R. Tolkien

As a salesperson, you probably pride yourself on being a "people person." You're friendly, outgoing and comfortable talking. But being a people person doesn't necessarily make you an effective communicator. What if your customer is *not* a people person?

I think many salespeople miss an opportunity to connect with their customers for one reason: They do not adjust their communication style to the style the customer prefers. Often the end result is that the message doesn't get through.

Once I had a disagreement with my wife and decided to use the silent treatment to try and make her feel bad about upsetting me (even though I was well aware that I was at fault for the disagreement). I maintained the silence for the entire evening, not speaking a word for hours.

At bedtime I realized I had a flight to catch at 7:00 a.m. My wife usually wakes me up early enough to catch the plane, but I didn't want to give in and break my silent treatment. So I wrote her a note: "Honey, will you please wake me up at 5:00 a.m.?" My wife rolled her eyes but took the note. I was delighted with myself. Without a word, I went to bed and slept like a baby.

When I awoke, I looked at the clock. It read 7:00 a.m. I missed my plane! Furious with my wife, I was ready to break the silent treatment when I saw a note on the pillow next to me. It read: "Wake up! It's 5:00 a.m.!"

The communication was timely and informative, but certainly not delivered in the manner I would have preferred. *Make sure your message is being delivered in the way your client needs to receive it.*

BEHAVIORAL FINGERPRINTING

How can we figure out what style of communication a client might prefer?

Dr. Tony Alessandra, a marketing strategist and applied behavioral scientist, has found that personality plays a key role in shaping how we like to talk, how we listen and interpret information, how we come to make a decision and how we connect with another person and come to like them.

Dr. Alessandra has identified a series of personality types and described their corresponding preferred style of communication. He worked with me to customize these descriptions to fit investment clients and the selling process. If you can identify a client's personality type, you can then determine the best communication style to use with the client.

We call this process "Behavioral Fingerprinting."

Investment clients typically fall into one of four dominant types of personalities:

- *The Relater*
- *The Socializer*
- *The Thinker*
- *The Director*

The Relater

The Relater is a people person. Relaters like to take time to get to know you and want you to know them. In meetings a Relater is more about building consensus than calling the shots.

Relaters' goals involve people issues. When they look at their investment portfolio, they see their retirement cottage at the lake, not a ledger balance. And they want you to see that, too.

A Relater would find you a cold person if you only discussed numbers, strategy and performance. Even though you may be doing an excellent job, the Relater will not be developing a strong relationship with you and may well leave you for an advisor he thinks better understands and cares about him and his values. Relaters are the ultimate example of the old adage: People don't care what you know until they know that you care.

You must adjust your communication to Relaters by taking time to get to know them and connect with them. When reviewing the progress of a Relater's investments, always refer to the people affected, i.e., "This will ensure that Mary has an adequate income should something happen to you."

If you engage in a Relater's life and values, he will be

much more likely to develop a lasting relationship with you, both as an advisor and a friend.

The Socializer

Like the Relater, the Socializer prefers to talk about people issues rather than numbers. But there is a critical difference between the two that will quickly become apparent.

Socializers tend to place themselves in the spotlight. They will want to share personal information or perhaps demonstrate their knowledge on a subject before getting down to business. Socializers need to know that they are important to the process and that they have made an intelligent choice.

Socializers also like to know about special services they are provided over and above the average client. Socializers like the additional attention and differentiation accorded them with "private client" services. Telling a Socializer she has qualified for the "platinum" level account will have meaning and value for her.

Make sure that this type of client has your total focus when you meet. Try to ensure that her experience is a special one; cater to her interests and treat her as the important client she is. Give a Socializer time in the spotlight before the meeting, and when you get down to business, make your presentation sizzle.

Overall, make sure you understand and focus on the issues that are important to Socializers, all the while making them feel important and valuable.

I am very well versed in the nuances of the Socializer because it is the category that best describes my own personality. For example, when I go to look at a new car, I don't care about the warranty information, the Consumer Reports recommendations or what a great value the car might be. I like to go for a drive, pass a glass-front building and look at myself to see if the car suits me! A salesperson focusing on things he believes are important might well miss the very key things I find critical in selecting a car.

The Thinker

The opposite of the Socializer is the Thinker. This is an individual who is focused on the numbers and the process. A Thinker is tactical. He needs specifics so he can analyze. He does not care for the short version or a "highlights" type of presentation.

When dealing with Thinkers you must offer a high level of detailed information so they can fully understand the decision you are asking them to make.

Thinkers want to know exactly what's on the agenda and like to be walked through the details. They're itching to get at the numbers. The more you engage in "chit-chat" the more the Thinker believes you are either avoiding the figures because they are bad or, even worse, that you don't know or understand the numbers.

If you are not a Thinker, it is critical that you adjust your communications style when interacting with this type of individual, since he will see you in an unfavorable light if you tend to gloss over data or offer the minimum amount of information. If you have a hypothetical example to share, then be prepared to explain the example, line by line, and describe the process for achieving the conclusions you are presenting. The more detailed the better when dealing with a Thinker.

The Director

The Director is also analytical by nature, but with a need to manage time. Directors are tactical, but at a bird's-eye level. They only have time for a summarized form of information. You should focus on the key numbers and essential details they need, without taking too much time to describe each process or dwelling too long on the number crunching you have done to achieve these conclusions.

The Director expects you to understand what she is looking for and to respect her time by offering the executive summary version of the information you want to share. Many corporate officers are Directors; they are comfortable receiving detailed but summarized reports. Doctors also tend to be pressed for time and appreciate summarized details and key points in an abbreviated format. Instead of a quarterly meeting, a Director may prefer a simple voice mail: "We're down for the quarter but up 7% for the year. I recommend no changes at this time. Call me with any questions."

By respecting the Director's time and being prepared and concise with your information, you send a loud and clear message that you understand her. She in turn will see you in a favorable light, as a person of intelligence and professionalism.

Understanding human behavior is critical to gaining trust, communicating effectively, building relationships that last and overcoming relationship anxiety. A client who feels you "get him" will have a much higher propensity to remain loyal to you. You can show you understand him by communicating in the style your client prefers, not necessarily in the style you prefer.

The Four Dominant Personalities

PERSONALITY	ORIENTATION	OPERATING STYLE	MEETING WARM UP	PREFERRED PRESENTATION
Relater	*Relationships*	*Consensus builder*	*"Let's chat a while before we talk business."*	*"Show me how others have done it."*
Socializer	*Relationships*	*Showman*	*"Let's talk about me first."*	*"Make it sizzle. Wow me!"*
Thinker	*Tactical*	*Analyzer*	*"Tell me exactly what the agenda is."*	*"Walk me through all of the details."*
Director	*Tactical*	*Decision maker*	*"No time for chit-chat, let's get down to business."*	*"Give me the top line. Now."*

CHAPTER FIVE

Absence makes the heart grow fonder of your competition

To Keep Your Clients, Keep in Contact

"Time is the most valuable thing a man can spend."
—Diogenes

The other day I heard a broker refer to a client as great because he didn't require much attention. In fact the broker hardly ever heard from him. I wonder how long that client will remain a client. Maybe he's already talking to a competitor. No news is not necessarily good news.

The strength of a relationship is proportional to the amount of time invested in it. How much time do you invest in your client relationships?

Most people tend to play customer contact by ear and handle communication on what they feel is an "as needed" basis. In other words, they only contact the customer when they have determined there is something significant to be shared or perhaps acted upon. Customers, for their part, only contact their sales rep when there is an issue or problem. This could mean that a very long time might pass with no contact at all. Then, when something does arise — usually a problem — you find yourself feeling out of touch and awkward. It's like running into an old girlfriend; you're not quite sure how she perceives the way you left things.

Your best clients want to hear from you more than once a month. This doesn't mean you need to *meet* with your client that often. You could spend time together socially. Or your contact can be via a phone conversation, voice mail message, e-mail, a personal note. But if you're not having some form of contact at least once a month, you're not building a lasting relationship — heck, you're barely maintaining a customer-vendor connection.

SHOW THEM YOU CARE

A broker I met in New England related the story of how he called every one of his elderly customers after a particularly heavy snowfall. Since he drove an SUV, he asked if he could bring them something from the store on his way home, or if they needed any other assistance since he was mobile. He said every client was not only gratified, but also surprised beyond his or her wildest expectations. Several of his customers replied that their own children had not called to check on them.

This broker had expressed his care and concern in a way that had nothing to do with money management or stock picking, but the effort was just as highly valued, if not more. Sometimes a small kindness or thoughtful gesture carries more weight than all the gold you could have spent.

Here are 12 ways you can show you care:

1. *Send a handwritten note.* Nothing beats it, whether it's to thank your client or to congratulate him. One caveat: don't misspell his name!

2. **Call with concern.** Did your client experience flooding in the storm? Is she worried about the down market? (Your reassurance in a down market will be appreciated. So will the fact that you're not hiding.)

3. **Send something.** It's not about the gift, but the gift of your attention. Send a book or article you came across and thought she'd enjoy, or give that hard-to-find jersey of his son's favorite team.

4. **Give a resource.** Maybe a client is in need of a medical specialist, a reputable contractor, a great place to buy cigars.

5. **Give your business.** If you want their loyalty, give them yours.

6. **Give a referral.** Send clients some business; it shows you respect their talents.

7. **Take an interest in their interests.** Don't fake it and don't force it, but if their hobbies intrigue you, ask them to help you get started.

8. **Recognize and respect.** Recognize dates and holidays that are important to them. Go to weddings, attend funerals, know and show proper respect for their religious observances.

9. **Follow up.** Show your attention to detail. Make sure a client has received what he requested. Ask if she has questions about what you presented. Set an appointment to go over the first monthly statement. Call after the first transaction confirmation has been sent.

10. **Touch base.** Find out how the anniversary dinner went, if the kids got settled at college, how the vacation was.

11. **E-mail.** NOT the latest chain letter or dirty joke, but

an e-zine or a link to a site they'd like.

12. ***Extend an invitation.*** Ask clients to an event you're involved with that will bring them enjoyment or at least enable them to meet prospects for their business. (Write a personal note on the invitation explaining why you thought of them.) Invite them to catch a game or concert, play golf, grab a drink or have dinner.

> *Keep a dozen assorted cards in your briefcase, along with your personal stationary and your address book. Remembering birthdays or anniversaries, expressing sympathy or sharing an idea takes only minutes to do, but speaks volumes to your customers.*

TAKE NOTES!

You know those people who always remember everyone's birthday? They send a card or call, and everyone else always says they're "so good at remembering." Well, how do you think they remember to send a card? They write it down! They have everyone's birthday written on their calendars or entered in their PDAs. They are no better at remembering than the rest of us. But they do care enough to write it down.

Put every client — in fact, every person you meet — in your contact file and write a couple of notes about them. When you're handed a business card, make notes on the back. Jot down their kids' names, their hobbies, favorite music, whatever. Then add to your notes every time you have contact with that person. Maybe he has back troubles, is looking for new porch furniture, or his daughter's birthday is this month — whatever comes up in conversation. Then the next time you are going to talk to him, refer to your file and you'll have something to ask about.

> "It's the little things that mean everything in life."
> —UNKNOWN

PART THREE

EXCELLING AT SERVICE

CHAPTER SIX

What you don't know can help you

Ask, Listen and Learn

"It's a healthy idea, now and then, to hang a question mark on things you have long taken for granted."

—BERTRAND RUSSELL

When I was a broker early in my career, one of my clients would always buy municipal bonds. Sometimes he'd call me with the specific issue he wanted to buy, and sometimes I'd call him when I learned certain bonds were available. He was investing $10,000 to $20,000 monthly, so I was enjoying a nice commission from the transactions.

About four years into the relationship, I read in a trading report that this client sold $3.5 million of Ralston Purina stock. I was shocked. This guy was a bond investor, not a stock investor. I quickly called him, hoping he might like me to invest the proceeds, but he had already invested it with another broker.

"Why didn't you tell me you owned stocks?" I asked.

His reply was simple: "You never asked."

LISTEN BEFORE YOU LEAP

Sometimes, in our excitement to meet a client's need, we miss an opportunity to provide a greater service if we had only probed and listened. In the investment business, an initial meeting is often driven by a transaction to fulfill a near-term need. Perhaps a client is seeking a higher rate of return on a maturing CD, or they have retirement assets rolling over and want your advice on investing this money.

Of course you want to solve the short-term problem. But many professionals never get beyond this level of service; the relationship is limited to that one transaction. Why? Because they don't ask their clients more questions and listen to the answers. Down the road, the professional ends up trying to guess at possible needs the client may have instead of making an effort earlier to find out.

Why not resist the urge to immediately solve the short-term problem and take the conversation to a broader focus? "Mr. and Mrs. Jones, I can certainly sell you any one of several products that might provide you with more income, but if you help me with some additional information, I may be able to do more for you."

This opens a door for finding out a great deal of information about your customers: what they have in total assets, how those assets are invested, the long-term needs for this money, short-term liquidity and potential short-term goals, transfer issues (estate or gift), or the need for accumulation of a larger nest egg to sustain the capital for a longer period of time.

Not only does asking and listening enable you to serve a client in other ways, it could very well enable you to better answer the need she came to see you about in the first place.

The hopes, dreams, aspirations and needs of the individual can provide a much better canvas on which to paint your professional opinion.

Gathering such information sets the tone of your working relationship going forward. It separates you from your product. It takes your relationship beyond the short-term situation you are going to help solve and establishes a future expectation of dialogue on other issues you may be able to help with.

THE NEED FOR FEEDBACK

Do you know why your customers buy from you? Do you know how they feel about the service and solutions your provide? Do you know what they expect from you? You may *think* you know. But in the immortal words of Will Rogers, "It's what we know that ain't so that gives us trouble."

Very rarely will clients tell you how you're doing without being prompted — especially if they don't think you're performing well. They'd rather avoid confrontation and, eventually, quietly leave you.

You must ask for feedback. You must be grateful for the answers and, of course, do something with the information. Being proactive and asking your clients for feedback has several benefits. You can:

- *Gain knowledge* (not just about serving that client but about serving that market segment)
- *Make additional contact* (always good)
- *Demonstrate that you care* (increasing trust)
- *Nurture a long-term relationship* (due to that trust)
- *Generate more business* (because you know how to satisfy the client's needs)

- *Increase the odds of getting referrals* (because satisfied clients tell friends)

ASK EARLY

Bill Cates, author of *Get More Referrals Now!*, suggests asking a prospect or new client this question (I've adjusted the time frame to better suit the investment business): "Let's pretend it's 20 years from today and we've been working together for that time. How will we know we've been successful? What's your measure of our success in working together?"

That is one terrific question. It's the kind of question that gains you valuable information and also helps to gain you something else: trust. Because by asking, you show the person that you care about your long-term relationship.

ASK OFTEN

Remember that when it comes to service, not only do different people have different perceptions and expectations, but the same person's perceptions and expectations can change over time. The bar will be raised or lowered (most likely raised) based on other buying experiences they have and on what is going on in their lives at the time.

To stay on top of clients' opinions and expectations of you, you must gather information on a regular basis — and not when the account hangs in the balance or you're looking to get more business out of them. Ask when the only reason you want to know is because you care.

Try asking, "How do you think I'm handling your needs on a scale of 1 to 10?" If it's an 8 or 9, ask: "How can I make it a 10?" If you get a 7 or below, you'll probably have to nudge some unexpressed complaints out of them: "Well, there's certainly room for improvement. Tell me, what things have left you less than thrilled?"

> "Zeal without knowledge is fire without light."
> —THOMAS FULLER

CHAPTER SEVEN

When they give you an inch, go the extra mile

Give More than Anyone Expects

"Your clients are happy when you meet their expectations.
Your clients become loyal when you exceed their expectations."

—BILL CATES

When a client gives you his business, he's giving you a chance. But getting the business is just the beginning; now you have to keep it. And to do that, you've got to "wow!" him.

Exceeding expectations is not about doing better than the other guy. The competitor you should worry about is the job you *could* have done. Fight mediocrity. Fight the willingness to do just enough to get by and nothing more. Successful people do more.

When you give customers superior service, you're changing the playing field. Now it's about their *total* experience, instead of just the product — which is good, because you can't always control the product, its cost or its performance. But what *is* in your control is *your* performance.

IMPROVE THE HUMAN CONDITION

Client service expert Barbara Glanz describes what she calls the human-business model. Every business interaction happens on two levels: the human level and the business level. The business level is about the work; the human level is about a client's feeling about the interaction. Clients have needs they want met in both categories. They'll probably tell you freely their business expectations (if you ask), but the emotional expectations? Well, here you have to make some presumptions.

You can certainly presume clients want to be treated with respect, friendliness and understanding. In addition, Steve Moeller, author of *Effortless Marketing for Financial Advisors*, says you'd do well to meet these five emotional needs:

- *To simplify*
- *To feel in control*
- *To feel secure*
- *To feel important*
- *To have fun*

By keeping these five needs in mind each time you interact with your clients, you'll ensure a positive association every time.

10 WAYS TO "WOW!"

Exceeding expectations is about more fully extending yourself to others and doing so with sincere enthusiasm. It might take a couple of extra minutes, but the payoff will be worth it. Here are 10 ways to wow your clients:

1. *Know their personal tastes and provide them.* Have their favorite soft drink or snack on hand in a meeting. Play the music they like.
2. *Call with status reports.* Even if it's to say you don't know yet.
3. *Introduce them to people in your office.* Especially those they'll likely have contact with. Your clients will be more comfortable and trusting of them, and the employees will be more apt to wow them when they meet the face behind the name.
4. *Don't just "hand them off" to customer service.* If a client calls you with a problem, *you* be the one to call customer service. The Ritz Carlton hotel staff is trained that whenever a guest asks how to get someplace in the hotel, they stop what they are doing and take them there personally. Give your clients Ritz service.
5. *Develop good relationships with your vendors.* Then you can ask for favors on behalf of your clients.
6. *Share your company's capabilities.* Remind clients of other services you can provide to help them.
7. *Take notice and compliment them.* Receiving validation on something we've personally selected or accomplished makes us feel good. (But only say it if you mean it.)
8. *Ask, "How am I doing?"* See Chapter 6.
9. *Be available outside 9 to 5.* Give them your cell and your home phone numbers.
10. *Help them out in another area of their lives.* Connect them with a trustworthy plumber. Find them a pet-sitter for their next trip.

Recognize that giving of yourself accomplishes even more than ensuring you keep clients. By giving more you'll become more influential to others. You will earn an impeccable reputation, which is the most valuable asset you can possess. Remember the old saying: The cream always rises to the top.

> "It's never crowded along the extra mile."
>
> —WAYNE DYER

CHAPTER EIGHT

Don't let molehills pile up into a mountain

Prevent Problems

"Do not look where you fell, but where you slipped."

—West African proverb

Never do we salespeople feel mightier than when we can make a big problem disappear for our clients. Everyone (including ourselves) is so impressed. We give a little "aw, shucks" and say we were glad to help, that's what we're here for.

But you know what else we're here for? To keep little things from piling up and turning into one big thing: a client leaving. I admit there's not as much glory in nipping little things in the bud. There are no great saves, no Hail-Mary passes. What is required are small efforts to sooth and satisfy, calm and cajole. But they must be done to prevent a real disaster.

As a case in point, let me share with you this cautionary tale:

> *Kathy Willings likes her investment advisor, Tom. For the most part, anyway. He's laid out an excellent long-term*

investment strategy for her. But he always ends up canceling and rescheduling their meetings at least once before they get together. And then he often forgets the hypotheticals he's promised to pull. Of course, that last meeting, who could really blame him; he was having such a bad day! Still, she just wishes he wouldn't promise things he can't turn around that quickly. And he takes forever to get back to her. Her friend Sam says she should tell Tom that these things bother her. But they're such minor things, really. She'd feel like she was being too trivial. Overall, he does a pretty good job. And she trusts him with her money, that's the important thing. Besides, Tom is the only investment advisor she knows...

What do you think is going to happen when sometime down the road Kathy Willings meets another investment advisor? She's going to leave Tom. She'll make some excuse about why she feels obligated to try this new advisor (such as he's the son of a dear friend). Tom will never know all the little reasons — the molehills that were so easily preventable.

PUT YOURSELF IN THEIR SHOES

It's not always easy to spot the molehills. If you aren't client-centered, you'll easily miss them. The best way to find the molehills is to walk around in your clients' shoes; consider the points of contact between your client and your company.

When a client calls and leaves a message about something she needs, how is it handled? Do you get back to her right away? Or does she have to wait days to know you even got the message? Is there someone at your office who can act as a concierge of sorts, directing calls, fulfilling small requests, letting customers know your availability in the next few days?

Likewise, what is the experience like for clients when they receive a bill or a performance statement? Is the statement so hard to decipher that they wonder if someone's trying to pull the wool over their eyes? Does the statement come from some third party and there's no contact with you? Is there a way you could add a connection through e-mail or a phone call — at least the first couple of times they get a new statement, to explain how to read it? Or could you walk them through a sample statement even before they receive their first one?

How do you think a client feels when the market is moving in a volatile fashion, especially if he doesn't hear from you during that time? Why not make a call to reassure him of the validity of your long-term strategy? Just because he isn't calling you in a panic doesn't mean he is okay with things. He might take your lack of contact as a sign that you don't care, or perhaps that you don't have confidence in what you have recommended. Don't be a "fair weather" advisor, only calling when the market is up and you have good news.

I recall vividly an extremely negative situation that developed early in my career. Our firm had recommended a particular growth stock that looked quite promising because of several new drugs that were being introduced. When the FDA delayed their production, the stock began to decline.

I spent several days and nights calling each customer I had placed in that stock (and several customers who I knew had purchased the stock through other brokerage firms). It was a tough call to make; the stock was down nearly 20%

from where most of my customers had purchased it. I explained the situation and the possible impact on the stock performance over the next several years. While they weren't happy with the news, my customers were appreciative of my concern and frankness. Whether they decided they were uncomfortable with further risk and sold, or they chose to continue to hold the stock in their portfolio, they were better informed and knew what to expect.

I became, for many of my customers, the only voice they were hearing and ultimately listening to. This was a key factor in my success, for as the markets turned and customers once again were adding money to their portfolios I didn't have to reestablish communication or credibility. We simply continued the solid and forthright relationship we had maintained.

10 OUNCES OF PREVENTION

Here are 10 ways to keep molehills from turning into mountains:

1. *Clarify expectations.* Don't assume you know what phrases like "as soon as possible" or "good returns" mean to your client.
2. *Anticipate needs.* Anticipate how you can be of service, whether it's for something little, like driving directions or a glass of water, or something big, like meeting an IRA rollover deadline.
3. *Simplify.* Make it easier for clients to get what they need from you, your company and the vendors you represent.
4. *Don't be late.* Don't make them wait for you or your deliverables.

5. *Solve a problem.* Even one you didn't create — especially one you didn't.

6. *Make them laugh.* Humor, especially the self-deprecating kind, puts people at ease and creates an atmosphere conducive to agreement.

7. *Be enthusiastic.* Show you are glad to be working with them. Don't complain about your job, the company, other clients or your schedule.

8. *Avoid misinformation.* Be up front with clients when you have bad news or don't know something. Don't tell half-truths.

9. *Empower them.* Explain your company's operating systems and show clients how to get the most satisfaction out of their interactions with the systems.

10. *Apologize when things go wrong.* It doesn't mean you have to admit fault (unless the fault really is yours). Then fix things, even when it's not your fault.

"The difference between what we do and what we are capable of doing would suffice to solve most of the world's problems."

—GHANDI

CHAPTER NINE

When a client has a bone to pick, get out a napkin

Handle Complaints Like the Opportunities They Are

"In the middle of a difficulty lies opportunity."

—ALBERT EINSTEIN

Pretend I'm your client and I've just called to complain: The mutual fund you put my money in isn't performing well and if you had returned my call last week, I could have told you to move my money into the fund my brother has and my shares would be worth more today.

Now quick, tell me what your initial reaction is: Do you feel defensive? ("I know more than his stupid brother.") Resigned? ("I'll just do what he wants.") Defeated? ("Darn, here goes another client.") How about thankful? *Thankful?!* YES!

Be thankful your client feels comfortable enough in your relationship to complain. Be thankful he's showing you he needs some personal attention. Be thankful he's talking to you right now instead of whining to others behind your back. Be thankful he's calling to complain and not to close his account. Be thankful for the chance to educate him on why your fund is better than the one his brother is in. Be thankful for the chance to solve a problem, to go through something negative with your client and come out the other side with a more solid relationship.

The Chinese word for crisis is made up of two characters: One means danger, the other means opportunity.

ENCOURAGE COMPLAINTS

According to a study performed by the Technical Assistance Research Programs Institute in Washington, D.C., clients who complain are more likely to continue doing business with you than clients who are unhappy but don't complain.

The bad news, according to the study, is that there's a propensity for dissatisfied clients not to complain. Let's clarify that: They won't complain to *you*, but you can bet they'll be giving their friends and family an earful. Wouldn't you rather they told it to you?

Some service experts cite the absence of complaints as a bad sign. Either the client is not being candid or he's not being contacted — both reflect a decline in the relationship.

Chances are if one client is having a problem, others are too. That's why it's so important to ask for feedback on a regular basis (see Chapter 6).

"We owe almost all our knowledge not to those who have agreed, but to those who have differed."

—CHARLES CALEB COLTON

A Problem Handled Well Strengthens the Relationship

I remember when my firm changed the format on our monthly statements. It was an improvement over the previous statement because more information was provided, but the format was radically different and many customers were confused by it. The first several weeks were a nightmare of calls from customers complaining about their statement and their aggravation in trying to find simple information. At first I was also upset. Why did we have to change and further complicate our lives? How could I sell when I was on the defense every day?

But out of this potentially huge lemon came sweet lemonade when an idea emerged. I began to proactively call my customers and ask for an appointment to review our new statement with them. Sometimes we did it in person, sometimes on the phone, but every time we each had a copy in front of us and walked through it line by line.

The result was happier customers and a great chance to review with them their holdings, what they own and why they own it. I saw things in their statements I hadn't really noticed before, whether it was idle cash or perhaps some stocks I wasn't aware they owned. This apparent crisis turned into a huge opportunity for improving customer relationships and generating more business.

A customer complaint or criticism is an opportunity to increase client loyalty, if you handle it correctly. Remember what we talked about in Chapter 1: E+R=O. The event doesn't equal the outcome — the event *plus your response* determines it.

10 Steps to Handling Complaints

When a client comes to you with a complaint, follow these steps in responding:

1. *Hear the person out without interrupting.* It'll be difficult for your client to express anger for more than a couple of minutes. When you interrupt, you allow him to refuel. Let him release all the steam so you can address the problem. Don't interrupt even with an apology — this can feel like you are trying to pacify him. He'll likely resent the action and the fact that he didn't get to completely get things off his chest.

2. *Lower your voice, stay calm and say, "I'm sorry."* These are the most powerful words you can say, so make them the first words out of your mouth. You're not admitting fault, you're merely sorry he is unhappy.

3. *Thank the client for sharing his feelings.* (Remember, better he share with you than a prospect.) Let him know you understand how he feels and that he has the right to feel that way.

4. *DON'T argue!* Even if you win an argument with a client, you don't win. Besides, a client's perception is his reality. Skip right over determining fault and get on with finding a solution.

5. *DON'T blame the system or get defensive.* Remember how it feels when you're the client. Would you rather have someone say, "I don't have anything to do with that" or, "Let's see what I can do to help"?

6. *Assure the client you will work to correct the problem.* And ask if he'll work with you to come up with an agreeable solution. Ask questions to gather more information, but make sure you listen carefully to all

of the responses. Don't just use the questions to calm him.

7. ***Establish the facts.*** Not only with your client, but also by talking with people in your company. Let the client know what you uncover.

8. ***Resolve the problem quickly.*** The faster you fix it, the less damage is done and the more the client is apt to continue working with you.

9. ***Thank the client again.*** Tell him you appreciate his bringing his problem or concern to your attention. This lets him know you value his opinions so he'll continue to tell you when something isn't right.

10. ***Follow up.*** Follow up to make sure the solution is implemented. Then follow up with your client to make sure everything is truly all right.

> "The first thing to do when you find yourself in a hole is to stop digging."
>
> —WILL ROGERS

PART FOUR

MARKETING YOURSELF

CHAPTER TEN

When you spread yourself too thin, you lose all your flavor

Pick Your Niche and Serve It Well

"Beware of dissipating your powers:
Strive constantly to concentrate them."

—GOETHE

You know the old saying "You can't be all things to all people." This is as true in sales as it is in the rest of our lives. Yet when it comes to our client base we salespeople tend to take everyone and anyone we can get. After all, why would we turn away business?

I'll tell you why you should: Because when you have too much of the wrong kind of business, it hampers your ability to serve your best accounts at the level they should be served.

When I was first starting out as a broker, I had a client who used to call me at least a dozen times a day for stock quotes on a dozen companies (back then there was no Internet or CNBC). He never wanted to buy any stocks, he never wanted to sell any. I was putting in an awful lot of hours on this client — reviewing his holdings, offering advice and making recommendations — but he never wanted to take any action that I suggested. I wasn't seeing any return on my investment of time.

One day I was having a particularly rough week and he was being particularly demanding. After I'd given him the prices on all the stocks he'd ask for (for the fifth time that day!), I thanked him for calling and then I said, "You know, I wish I had five clients just like you."

"You do?" he asked. "But all I ever do is ask for stock quotes. You're not making any money off me."

"I know," I responded. "That's why I wish I had five clients like you — right now I've got 10."

You should be focusing on a client base that makes the best use of what you have to offer — your training, talents and experience. We all know the 80/20 Rule: 80% of revenue comes from 20% of your customers. If you want to maximize your income you need to work with more clients who are like your top 20%.

Know Who You Want to Attract

So who are your best clients?

In the investment industry, you might assume your best clients are those who made a lot of trades over the last year; they generated the most revenues for you.

But I'll argue that it's better to focus on the *potential* in your book of clients. Many of the customers you now have on your books have far more potential than you've realized thus far. If you only measure your clients based upon the revenues they have generated, you will continue to miss this hidden opportunity to provide your services.

To measure a client's potential, look at the their financial net worth. Why? Because the complexity of a person's financial situation increases with their net worth, and their need for advice and direction increases in proportion. Focus your advice and guidance on those people who need or have likelihood of needing more of what you have to offer.

Years ago, there was a well-known bank robber by the name of Willy Sutton. Anxious to learn what motivates a person like Sutton, someone asked him, "Why do you rob banks?" Without hesitation he responded, "Because that's where the money is." As salespeople, we need to look at where the money is. That's where the opportunity lies.

Segment Your Clients, Segment Your Efforts

Not all clients are worth your full attention. And some are worth more than you may be giving. To know where to focus your attention, first evaluate your clients' performance and potential.

Think about the 10 clients you spend the most time with or working for. Jot down their names. Next to their names, using a scale of 1 to 5 (1 being low and 5 being high), rate each on two criteria: their net worth and their propensity to invest. (Consider doing this exercise with *all* your clients. You'll find it enlightening.)

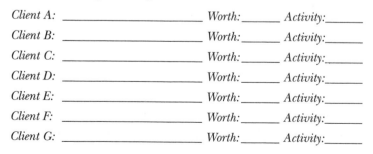

Client A: _____ *Worth:* _____ *Activity:* _____

Client B: _____ *Worth:* _____ *Activity:* _____

Client C: _____ *Worth:* _____ *Activity:* _____

Client D: _____ *Worth:* _____ *Activity:* _____

Client E: _____ *Worth:* _____ *Activity:* _____

Client F: _____ *Worth:* _____ *Activity:* _____

Client G: _____ *Worth:* _____ *Activity:* _____

Client H:	_____	Worth:_____	Activity:_____
Client I:	_____	Worth:_____	Activity:_____
Client J:	_____	Worth:_____	Activity:_____

Now, plot your clients on the following graph according to their numbers for net worth and investment activity.

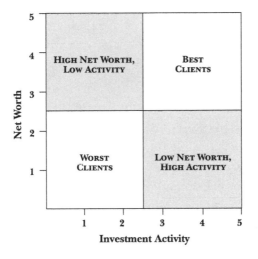

Let's look at the worst case first: clients with low net worth and low activity. *Your "D" level clients.* Not only do you make considerably less on these clients, you also spend proportionally more time on them. Consider letting them go; refer them to a newcomer in your agency who has a smaller book and lots of time to spend. Although it will feel strange to walk away from business, you truly can't afford to keep servicing these accounts — it's time that could be used servicing or attracting "A" clients. Sometimes you have to turn down the good to make room for the great.

For your "C" clients, who have low net worth but are active in the market, you could try to find ways to grow their net worth. Show them a more aggressive savings program, introduce them to clients who may be able to help grow their business, send them a referral. But you don't want to spend too much time with them. Minimize your service effort. You need that time for your "B" and "A" accounts.

For "B" clients — your high net worth, low activity accounts — focus on ways to increase their investing activity and upgrade them to "A" client status. Consider conducting a needs analysis to help these clients better understand what they are missing. Learn what their objections and apprehensions are. Share success stories. Invite them to functions with some of your best clients.

Your "A" clients have a high net worth and high investment activity. You want to keep them happy. You want to stay in touch with them. You also want to *duplicate* them.

DEVELOP AN IDEAL CLIENT PROFILE

Make a list of all your clients with top potential, the "A" clients in terms of net worth and investment activity. Now cross off anyone who is extremely difficult to work with, anyone you just don't share an affinity with, and anyone you don't enjoy working with. Just because they have money doesn't mean they're worth it (yes, it's true!). These people can be on your "B" list but not your "A" list, not the list you want to clone and increase.

Next, look for niches to classify your clients. Are there segments of certain professions, like doctors or attorneys, or key employees in large or fast-growing companies? Are there groups of retired couples? Independent, single older women? Successful entrepreneurs? Divide and list your "A" clients into these segments. Defining and targeting niches make it easier to create word of mouth, to obtain referrals and even to cold-call a prospect.

Now list the common traits of your best clients within each segment. Think about both the demographic descriptors (age, occupation, location, family situation) as well as psychographic (personality type, risk tolerance, general attitude toward money and life). A prospect should have both the financial need and the desire for help.

Write down a profile of your perfect client for each segment, five or six bullet points that describe this person. Use this profile to qualify leads and help you recognize ideal clients. In addition you can omit dollar amounts and share this profile with your existing clients and other referral sources. That's right, verbally share the description of the people whom you are best able to serve so they have a concrete picture of whom you're looking for. When you identify and ask for what you want, you usually get it.

Sample Profile: Physicians/Surgeons

Perhaps you've identified that a few of your "A" clients are physicians or surgeons. An ideal prospect profile for that segment to share with referral sources might look like this:

- *Respected and influential in the field*
- *Established, successful practice*
- *55 years or older*
- *Married, never divorced*
- *Good business sense*

When targeting a niche, try some targeted research. Conduct informational interviews with your clients in a particular segment and with persons of influence in that segment. Be sure you understand what they value, need and desire — in investing and in life.

CHAPTER ELEVEN

Ride in on a horse of a different color

Differentiate Yourself

"I always wanted to be somebody; I should have been more specific."
—LILY TOMLIN

Everyone likes to be the knight in shining armor, riding in on the white horse to save the day. The problem is, there are 100 knights on white horses ready to help every prospect. To stand out, you need to ride in on a horse of a different color. You need your solution to go beyond the generic to the specific. You need to differentiate yourself.

When I was first starting out in the investment business, I was a broker for Merrill Lynch. I thought having my name on that company business card was my ticket to sell to anyone. After all, I was a professional with the leading investment firm. What more did I need to say? One day I called on an executive with a firm based in Richmond, Virginia. His secretary didn't seem to be as impressed with my calling card as I was.

"He doesn't see anyone without an appointment," she said.

"He'll see me," I said confidently. "I'm with Merrill Lynch."

After much cajoling, she finally agreed to take my business card in to him. I confidently sat on the leather sofa in the reception area and waited for him to call me in to handle all of his investing. But instead, his secretary came out and returned my card to me torn in two pieces. I couldn't believe it.

"Hey, these cards are expensive!" I said. "Tell your boss he owes me five cents."

Though she strongly advised against it, I insisted she go in and tell him I said he owed me a nickel. When she returned and handed me the coin, I pulled out another card and said, "Tell him today only, they're two for a nickel."

Now, you could say I differentiated myself to that prospect — I was certainly memorable, albeit not in a positive way. I didn't articulate a single point of value to him. What I needed was the ability to communicate to my prospect what I could do for him that was advantageous to his goals. Even though I showed up, I failed to show my competitive advantage.

IDENTIFY YOUR COMPETITIVE ADVANTAGE

If I asked you to describe to me why you are different and better than your competition, what would you say? When I ask this question in the seminars I lead, invariably most people start telling me their credentials: their track record, the years of experience they have, how much in assets they manage, etc.

To each point I respond, "So what?"

I'm not belittling their qualifications, but I am challenging them to tell me why it is important to me. We tend to describe ourselves in comparison to the competition instead of focusing on why what we offer is important to the customer. How does what you offer serve your client's needs and values?

The answer is in your *Competitive Advantage Statement* (or CAS) — a few sentences that crystallize the benefit of working with you. Your Competitive Advantage Statement must:

- *Address the primary concerns of your "A" client base*
- *Emphasize what makes you different*
- *Overcome or preempt common objections you encounter*
- *Complement the corporation's positioning or at least not conflict with it*
- *Be short and memorable, so clients can repeat it to others*

When prospects see how your focus meshes with their priorities, they'll be more apt to become clients. When clients understand your unique value, they'll be more likely to stay loyal to you. Knowing your competitive advantage also enables clients to become a great source of referrals as they share your message with their friends, colleagues or relatives.

Sample Competitive Advantage Statements

Here's my professional Competitive Advantage Statement:

> *"I specialize in serving the unique needs of financial services reps. I've had a lot of success coaching them in how to build thriving long-term practices. Having been in this industry since 1966, I bring a long-term perspective; I've witnessed firsthand the differences between highly successful*

pros and the not so successful ones. I've observed that those at the top of the list, year after year, secure a loyal book of clients and follow certain best practices. "

By ending with the topic of loyal clients and best practices, I set up two logical questions from the listener: How does one secure a loyal book? And what best practices do I recommend following? I've initiated a conversation.

Here's an example of a great Competitive Advantage Statement from a financial professional in Florida:

"I specialize in serving the unique needs of the retired community and in doing so I have been highly successful in helping my customers preserve their lifestyle in these difficult times. Perhaps you, like many of my best customers, at one time felt comfortable managing your own money in the bull market. However, today my clients tell me they find great comfort and value in the personalized approach I take to guiding their investments in these volatile times. I'd be interested in hearing your thoughts. "

Notice that in the CAS above the phrase "in these difficult times" anticipates the objection of "I can do this myself," and then goes on to answer it with the next sentence. In my CAS, I bring up my long-term perspective as a preemptive strike against the objection "I've been doing this awhile, I know the ropes."

Write Your Own Competitive Advantage Statement

Now it's time to write your own Competitive Advantage Statement. If you've identified more than one market segment of "A" clients in Chapter 10, you'll want to craft a Competitive Advantage Statement for each segment, even if each CAS differs only slightly. Here are the steps:

1. *Select a target market.*
2. *Identify the primary concern of your market (their problem, goal or fear).* Try to include how they feel about the issue.
3. *Describe how you've answered their concern.* Emphasize your unique talents and your success on your clients' behalf.
4. *Make a preemptive strike against common objections.*
5. *Close with an intriguing point.* It will open the door for more conversation.

Write your statement and memorize it. If you don't know your competitive advantage, how do you expect others to?

TELL A ONE-LINER

Once you have your Competitive Advantage Statement, condense the overall message into a single-sentence benefit statement. This benefit statement is like a verbal billboard: You'll use it when you only have a short time to share a compelling statement. Perhaps you're on the golf course or at a cocktail party and someone asks what you do for a living. Instead of saying, *"I'm a stockbroker"* or, *"I manage investments,"* you'll say something like:

"I help retirees preserve their lifestyles with smart investment choices."

"I help entrepreneurs manage their personal investments — I grow their money while they're busy growing their businesses."

My personal one-liner is:

"I help financial service reps develop a long list of long-term loyal clients."

Notice how the benefit statement identifies a market segment and links the salesperson with a key benefit valued by his market. It refers to results, not product or process. A good one-liner should invite questions and make someone want to hear more. It's also conversational — in fact, don't be afraid to have fun with the line and your delivery of it.

The one-liner does *not* minimize your talents (as just giving your title does), ramble on (either floundering for a focus or expounding because you love your subject) or try to impress (name-dropping, positioning yourself above everyone else).

For each segment you've identified in Chapter 10 and written a CAS for, now craft and memorize a benefit one-liner.

BE YOUR OWN BRAND

Remember that people buy *you*, not your products. And whether you realize it or not, you are your own brand. How you dress, how you act, what you do, what you choose — everything reflects your brand.

It's funny, but often the very things that make people interesting are the things they tuck away when they're in "professional mode." Stop that!

As I've said, people want to do business with friends — and you can't become friends if you're not sharing yourself. Worse, if you don't give clients adequate personal information, they'll probably form a shallow impression of you, possibly even a stereotype. It is a fact that people will form opinions of you based on the information available. Make your information available.

There is a grocer in Western Pennsylvania who is known far and wide for his style of dress. At parties he's the one in the custom-tailored canary-yellow suit with shoes dyed to match. Perhaps you wouldn't be caught dead dressed like that and would not want your personal brand to be the Wild Dresser. But I'll tell you one thing: People everywhere know who this guy is.

Of course, much more goes into a brand than just the way you dress or your interests and hobbies. The way you treat customers, your response/follow-up time, your integrity, your willingness to be a resource to them — professionally and personally — all of these things and more go into forming your personal brand. Once people meet and do business with the Wild Dresser, they discover that this person who continually attracts attention for his dress is also a person who constantly shines the spotlight on the accomplishments of others.

Define Your Brand

You can write your own statement of your brand. If the Wild Dresser were to write his own brand statement, I bet it'd be something like: "I am memorable in all aspects of my life." And from his appearance to his customer service, he is.

I know an insurance professional whose brand statement might be: "I am the Go-To Guy for everyone in my life." Whether a client has a claim, wants advice, or needs a recommendation for an orthopedic surgeon, this guy is the man to call. He has built up a tremendous network, which he never hesitates to share with his clients (just like we talked about in Chapter 3). Because of this, he has tremendous value in his clients' lives and they are loyal to him.

Developing your brand is *not* about creating a false image of who you are or what you do. Don't try to be something you're not. If you're not good at following up and following through, you certainly want to work on improving, but don't try to make it your brand. It'll never fly.

Branding yourself is about developing and making known your talents and personality characteristics. Determine what your best character traits are and how you can put those to use for the good of others.

Stedman Graham, author of *Build Your Life Brand!*, says that defining and building your brand helps you build a life that people remember, respect and honor long after you are gone. Who of us doesn't want that?

"Be distinct or be extinct."

—TOM PETERS

CHAPTER TWELVE

Out of sight, out of mind, out of business

Position Yourself to the Prospects You Want

"In sales, it's not who you know, it's who knows you."
—Jeffrey Gitomer

If you've read Chapters 10 and 11, you've identified your market niches and you've honed your message and personal brand. Now, how will you reach your niche with your message? How will you keep yourself top-of-mind, so when prospects need investment services they'll think of you?

The first and foremost approach is through relationships. This includes referrals and networking, which I cover separately in Chapters 13 and 14. But there is another way of reaching your audience, an indirect approach involving *building credibility.*

With this approach, your overriding goal is to position and promote yourself as a resource — an expert on the topic (and a highly referable one at that). *In this realm you are not a salesperson, you are a knowledgeable resource* looking to give help freely and without expectation.

There are several activities you can do to build your credibility:

Research Niche Associations

In the United States, there are more than 34,000 trade and professional associations, non-profit organizations and community groups. Many of these associations publish formal newsletters, have resource websites, hold regular meetings and seek outside presenters for programs. Connect with the right groups and you connect with your ideal prospects.

Your local library has the *Encyclopedia of Associations*, which lists associations for every industry and affinity group. You can also find directories and association websites by searching on the Internet.

If possible, join an association; participating is promoting. But even if you aren't a member, you can become a resource for their members by offering to speak, write an article for the newsletter, etc. You must be willing to give freely and expect no payment, but in doing so you will build your reputation as an expert on your subject as it relates to their concerns.

Get a By-Line

Contribute articles to print or online publications that reach your various market segments. To break in, focus on local publications or national pubs with small circulations. You can research these on google.com or yahoo.com. For example, I searched on "resources for widows" and found www.widownet.org, which has a financial section on their site. From there, I could contact the organization and offer to write an article for the website. You might also try to get your own column in a trade publication or newsletter that reaches your target audience.

A radio-show segment is also an opportunity. Years ago I was working with Signet Investment Corporation in Richmond, Virginia. During the 5:00 p.m. drive-time evening news on WRVA, I would give the stock market report. The show's host would even ask me a couple of questions. I had several listeners become clients from that radio awareness. I know an investment rep in Dallas who had a similar segment on the public radio station and it grew into a call-in show.

Self-Publish

Write special reports, whitepapers or booklets and make them available to clients and prospects in your target niches.

Write a column and distribute it via e-mail. Encourage people to forward it and include a link for others to get on the mailing list. Writer Bruce Cameron built up enough readership of his e-column on parenting teenagers that he was able to get a book deal, then a TV show, for "8 Simple Rules for Dating My Teenage Daughter."

Write a blog (a web log). A blog is your own space on the Internet where you share your insights and knowledge. You post new entries as often as you like, and you can link to various websites and online resources you think your readers will find interesting. Find out more at www.blogger.com.

Present Educational Events

People like to learn; it helps them feel more in control of their lives. One of the top qualities investors look for in investment advisors is the ability and willingness to educate them. Offering an educational event — a seminar, a workshop, a panel discussion — will establish you as an expert in your field. And if you customize the education for a particular target segment — "Tax Strategies for Doctors," for example — you'll position yourself as an expert in serving their industry. Educational events are a great way to connect with clients and meet new prospects. Invite your clients to bring colleagues or friends who could benefit from the knowledge.

SPEAK AT SPONSORED MEETINGS

Instead of you or your company hosting an event, consider speaking at another organization's event. (Too nervous to speak in public? Do it once and you'll be over it, honest.)

Make yourself known (via a media kit and/or a phone call) to trade and affinity associations, educational institutions, professional organizations, philanthropic organizations, community groups and chambers of commerce. The program chairs for these groups have speaking slots to fill. They are looking to add value to their meetings for the members. They may also be looking to raise money (you could charge a fee and donate it back to the organization). The organization will promote the event, thereby increasing your visibility and credibility. They are, in effect, endorsing you.

COLLECT EVALUATIONS (AND NAMES)

Wherever you speak, you should always use an evaluation form. Hand them out or leave them on the chairs, but do ask people to fill them out. The forms help refine your presentation based on feedback from the audience. They also enable you to collect names and phone numbers of prospects without irritating people. Your evaluation form should consist of five parts:

1. *Contact info* — Name, address, e-mail, phone, preferred form of contact. If they don't want you to know, they simply won't fill it out.

2. *Evaluation* — Ask them to rate the workshop overall and in terms of information value and effective presentation. You can also ask a few open-ended questions: what they wish you spent more/less time on, the most important concept they took away, and how you can improve the program.

3. *"May I quote you?"* — They check "yes" or "no."

4. *Referral* — "Do you know someone who would be interested in or benefit from this presentation?" (Name, organization, phone number.)

5. *Lead qualifier* — They can check boxes for "I'd like to meet with you as soon as possible," "I'm not sure I'm interested/I have questions, call me," "I may be interested in the future, call me on _____," and "No thanks, I'm not interested."

It's fine if you don't get every attendee's name. Not every attendee is a prospect. Your goal is to encourage interested people to identify themselves.

CHAPTER THIRTEEN

A bird in the hand can show you two in the bush

Prospect for Referrals

"Do what you do so well that your customers come back
and bring their friends."

—WALT DISNEY

The word *referral* makes a lot of salespeople uncomfortable for no good reason. If you believe in your product and
you believe that you provide a valuable service, why would
you want to deprive your clients' friends and associates of it?

If you feel hesitant about asking for referrals, consider
whether it is because you don't really believe you're giving
clients the best you can. If that's true, there's a simple solution: Start giving your best. (Practically every chapter in this
book demonstrates a way to do just that.)

When you are giving your best, when your service is truly
of value — when your relationship is something clients
appreciate and rely on — there's no reason they won't give
you a referral. In fact, you may not even have to ask for it.
When you develop relationships and regular interaction the
right way, referrals become less about you asking for a favor

and more about you *giving* a favor, letting more people come into the fold of your service.

Here's a real-life illustration of the perfect way a referral should happen (and did):

An insurance agent and financial advisor are strategic partners; they refer business to each other all the time. They are both involved in an annual charity motorcycle ride for the Make-a-Wish Foundation. The insurance broker rides his motorcycle, while the financial advisor delivers and serves food and refreshments to the riders at one of the stops along the five-hour ride.

At this particular stop, the insurance agent is eating with one of his clients, a car dealer, whom he invited to ride. It's the car dealer's first year riding in the event and he's asking his insurance agent how he came to be involved. The agent points to his friend serving the food and says that he got him involved. "We refer a lot of business to each other; he manages the 401(k) plans for a lot of my clients' companies — handles the enrollments personally."

"Oh really?" says the car dealer. "Does he handle any car dealerships? I've been thinking about switching providers."

The insurance agent says, "Yes, actually he specializes in car dealerships," and mentions the dealerships the advisor writes.

"Great," says the auto dealer. "Can you introduce me to him?"

The insurance agent walks the auto dealer over, introduces him to the investment advisor, and the two end up exchanging business cards and agreeing to have lunch next week.

That's the power of referrals. In this case the referral was from a strategic alliance, but it could have just as easily been from a client. Don't you want to infuse your business with that kind of power?

What's in It for Them?

Keep in mind that a referral doesn't only benefit you. It also benefits the person giving it. If the referral comes from a strategic alliance, as in the above story, your service gives them another opportunity to serve their clients. Likewise, when your clients refer friends to you, they are helping them. In addition, clients will give you referrals because they want to help *you.* If you've been serving them well and helping them, they'll take pleasure in helping you.

All You Have to Do is Ask — and Sometimes You Don't Even Have to Do That!

Asking for referrals follows the 80-20 rule: 80% of clients would give you a referral. Only 20% are ever asked!

The key is *when* to ask for the referral.

My wife bought a set of knives from a young woman who was selling them through in-home presentations. We needed a new set of knives, and these seemed to be of good quality. After the woman closed the sale, she asked my wife for the names of friends and family she could call on. It made my wife feel uncomfortable and she declined to do so. The problem was, the saleswoman was asking for the names too soon. My wife hadn't yet experienced the value in what she had been sold.

A few months went by, and the woman called on my wife again, to see if she liked the knives and was interested in buying more. By now, my wife had used the knives and loved them — in fact, she'd been raving about them to several of her friends. My wife not only bought a set of steak knives, she also gave the saleswoman the phone number of two friends who had mentioned they really needed new knives.

Bill Cates, author of *Get More Referrals Now!*, says, "The time to ask for a referral is when value has been given and value has been recognized."

Clients are recognizing your value when they tell you they are so glad you came along, that you really have the perfect solution or that they've learned so much from you. Now is the time to say something like, "I'm glad I could help. This is the kind of work I really enjoy, so if you know of anyone else who could use my services, I hope you'll pass my name along."

Statements like this lay the groundwork, letting clients know you appreciate referrals and are interested in more business. As odd as it may sound, sometimes clients aren't aware that you like to get business through referrals. And sometimes they assume their friends might be too "small" for your interest. Letting them know you grow your business through referrals opens the door for conversation.

Even after laying the groundwork, there may come a time you actually need to come out and ask a client for a name. When the rapport is there and they've recognized your value, say something like, "I seem to be at my best helping clients like you, specifically, people who…. Do you know anyone I might talk to?"

Help Them Help You

Your clients and strategic partners can be part of your sales force and you don't have to pay them a penny in commission. But you do need to let them know whom you are looking for and remind them what you can provide these prospects.

When your customers talk to friends and associates about why they do business with you, what do you think they say? They probably don't say as much as you'd like them to. You can affect this process by teaching them a better way to describe your uniqueness. You can help them help you by explaining why you are different.

Of course you've prepared, by developing the market segmenting we talked about in Chapter 10 and the Competitive Advantage Statement we talked about in Chapter 11. Don't just use these tools with new prospects — share them with existing clients so they know your vision.

Imagine if the knife saleswoman had determined that her ideal customer was a woman who was an empty nester, who likely had relied on the same set of kitchen knives for decades and deserved a new set (and could afford it now that the kids were on their own). When my wife raved about the knives, the saleswoman could have said something like, "My most satisfied customers are women like you: Once they use the new knives, they realize just how dull their old knives have become after decades of cooking for their families. Do you know anyone else like yourself who might be ready for — and, frankly, deserving of! — a new set of knives?"

Remember to also share your benefit one-liner. That way they can easily describe your competitive advantage to their friends, relatives and associates.

Get Introduced

Your client has identified a friend who could use your services. Now what? Well, put yourself in the prospect's shoes: How would you feel if you got a call from a salesperson saying, "Your friend so-and-so suggested I call you." Do you wonder for a moment if your friend really did give your name to the salesperson? Do you try to remember if your friend has said they actually like working with this person? Do you worry your friend might have given your name to get this salesperson off his back (and forgot to tell you to just blow the guy off)?

There are better approaches to getting an introduction. An easy one is to ask your client to e-mail the prospect and copy you on the message. After the prospect has received the e-mail, wait a day or two and then write to ask if he'll take your call and what time would be best for him.

Of course, the best way to get introduced is in person. If your client and the prospect know each other well, offer to take them to lunch or breakfast. Or see if your client will take you to an event for an association that he and the prospect both belong to. You can also invite your client and prospect to an event or activity as your guest.

Do Your Homework

Before you meet the prospect, please, do your research. My friend Michael Salmon, author of *SuperNetworking for Sales Pros,* says you should be able to answer the following five questions *before* you meet a prospect (you can substitute an individual for the company):

1. *What does the company do and in what industry?*
2. *In which areas does the company need help?*

3. *What is my (and my company's) value to this company?*
4. *Who in the company (or industry) would realize and appreciate my/our value proposition?*
5. *What do I offer that is quantifiable and makes me and my product/service stand out from the crowd?*

Where do you find this information? From the person who gave you the referral, people who've worked with the company or your prospect, the Internet, the company website and association members.

Most salespeople don't bother to do their homework — so imagine the impression you'll make on your prospect if you do.

CHAPTER FOURTEEN

Birds of a feather flock together — where are you?

Network to Net More

"Successful people are interdependent, not independent."
—Richard Weylman

How many times have you said, "I can sell them if I could only meet them!"

How do you try to meet them? It has always amazed me to watch how much time, effort and money the average salesperson will spend on prospecting groups of people. Sometimes expensive lists are purchased, then nice letters are sent out, then calls are made, and out of 100 such contacts, maybe two or three appointments are set. This isn't a bad way to go, but it is undoubtedly a slow one if you want to grow your business.

The better approach by far is networking. When I say networking I don't mean schmoozing and glad-handing. I mean creating meaningful relationships with people who can help you and whom you can help — be they in your target market, your field, associated fields or circles of interest.

How do you build such a network? I'm glad you asked!

You gotta follow the rules:

RULE #1: YOU GOTTA GO

Woody Allen said that 80% of life is just showing up. While there's much more to networking than just showing up, attendance is a good place to start. At the end of a long day, it's so tempting to skip that association dinner or networking event. But networking is like the lottery: You've got to play to win — and the odds are a zillion times better with networking.

The idea here is to seek out your best prospects where they prefer to be. Ask your top clients what organizations they're involved in. Go to business events, social and cultural events, civic and charity events. Go to conferences, workshops and seminars — those that interest you and those that interest your prospects.

When it comes to networking, remember to:

- *Go often.* You must remain visible. Keep your calendar full of social engagements, conferences and events.
- *Go early and stay late.* The longer you stay the more contacts you'll meet.
- *Go it alone.* If you go with a friend, split up or you'll divide your concentration and dilute the benefit.
- *Go to work.* Get around to meet a lot of people. At an event with 100 people, you could speak to half of them and probably make 30 contacts.
- *Go to help.* Get involved in the organizations you belong to! Help organize the event. Or speak at the event.

Rule #2: You Gotta Gather

Bring people together. Don't be afraid to mix business with pleasure, professional with personal.

There are a great many ways to bring people together. You can plan a golf outing for many clients (who can bring prospects). Host a purely social event your clients would enjoy and encourage them to invite a few friends (an art show, a concert, a restaurant opening, a hospitality tent at an auto show). You can also organize an event within an event: a dinner during a conference, a pre- or post-happy hour connected to an industry networking event.

The average broker holds a seminar on investing, the market, or perhaps on the economy and interest rates. The exceptional broker also offers seminars on other subjects of interest to his best customers. For example, a broker could sponsor a book signing with a popular author and offer refreshments in cooperation with the bookstore seeking to sell more books.

How about approaching a high-end auto dealership with an idea to cosponsor an event showcasing the new models? They'll invite their list of customers, you invite your best clients, and you both meet a lot of new prospects.

An insurance agent in Pittsburgh holds Steelers tailgate parties that have become almost legendary. Among other things, he has a custom-painted utility truck with beer taps built into the side. He grills steak and seafood kabobs. It's a chance to hang out with clients, as well as meet the friends they bring along to show off the impressive event their agent hosts. This same agent hosts an annual bonfire and hayride at his farm, geared toward children even though he doesn't have any. It's held the same Saturday every year and clients know they have a standing invitation for their families as well as friends.

I heard a great idea from a broker who consistently is in the top rankings of his firm for new accounts. He said that he first came across this idea by accident, but it has since become a regular practice. A good customer of his asked if his firm could buy a table at a fundraiser for the American Cancer Society. The night of the event, two couples coming from the firm had to cancel. The broker started calling customers and found two couples with no plans for the evening. In addition to the great food and entertainment, the broker spent quality time with his clients and met several people the clients knew at the event. He mixed and mingled and ended up with over 50 highly qualified prospects. No business was discussed, but he did ask everyone he met a lot of questions about themselves. He kept in contact and eventually opened a dozen new accounts.

I attended an impressive event where several different companies got together in a combined effort to meet more people. A builder of high-end homes, a jeweler, an estate planning expert, a luxury auto dealer and a wine merchant together hosted an open house featuring a wine-tasting with light hors d'oeuvres. It was an enjoyable evening for everyone and certainly a big success for the presenters; they were able to meet over 100 new prospective customers for their products and services. They understood that birds of a feather like to flock together, and they made sure they were part of the flock.

RULE #3: YOU GOTTA GIVE

When it comes to networking, the same rule applies as

it does to all of sales (all of life, really): Give without expectations. Make your first concern be what you can give to people, how you can help them.

When you are first meeting someone, and you don't yet know how you might help them, you can give them your attention and interest, and that's giving plenty. Everybody's deepest desire is to be significant and be recognized. Ralph Waldo Emerson once said, "Every man I meet is my superior in some way. In that, I learn of him." Everyone has something to teach us. You must be in a frame of mind where you truly want to hear a person's story and don't care if you get to share yours.

When you really listen to someone's story — their passions, their wants, their needs (personal as well as professional) — you might find all sorts of ways you can be of service to them. Three areas that are particularly strong bonds for people are health, financial well-being and family. When you assist someone with a health concern, improve their financial situation or take an interest in their children (or, for some people, their parents or their pets), you connect on a fundamental level that can create loyalty.

Remember the words of the immortal Dale Carnegie (and I paraphrase here): You can be more successful in two months by becoming really interested in other people's success than you can in two years trying to get other people interested in your own success.

Networking events are not the time to be selling your wares. The sales part comes later. For now, your only goal is to establish a connection. After the event, quiz yourself. Did you:

- *Listen actively and generously?*

- *Find a reason to connect with each contact later?*
- *Step out of your comfort zone to connect with new people?*
- *Approach people with an attitude of giving and look for ways to give without expectation?*

RULE #4: YOU GOTTA GALVANIZE

After making a connection with someone at an event, you must follow up if you are to build a relationship. If you don't follow up, you fail — you fail to be remembered, you fail to keep the connection, you fail to make them part of your life (and that's the point after all, isn't it?).

Luckily, it's never been easier to follow up, thanks to e-mail. Drop a note saying how nice it was to meet them and you'd like to keep in touch. Then put a reminder in your organizer or PDA to contact them in a couple of months.

Keith Ferrazzi calls this ongoing follow-up of quick, casual greetings "pinging." Here are his pinging rules of thumb, as outlined in his book *Never Eat Alone*:

- *When you're working to create a new relationship:* the person needs to see or hear your name in at least three modes of communication (e-mail, phone call, face-to-face, etc.) before there is substantive recognition.
- *Once you've gained some recognition:* you must nurture the developing relationship with a phone call or e-mail at least once a month.
- *If you want to turn a contact into a friend:* you need a minimum of two face-to-face meetings out of the office. Meet for coffee, breakfast or dinner. Find them at an event or a conference. Share a hobby or interest (golf, sporting events, etc.).

- *To maintain a secondary relationship:* ping two to three times a year.

Remember that networking is a long-term strategy. It takes time to establish trusting relationships. That's why you don't wait to start networking when business is bad and you need prospects — you've got to build it before you need it. Even if you have all the business you can handle right now, now is a great time to network. You won't be feeling desperate and you'll easily be able to stay in the giving mindset.

PART FIVE

GOING BEYOND

CHAPTER FIFTEEN

DO
NOT
DISTURB!

Leave well enough alone and you'll never know what could have been

Keep Growing

"Everything you want is just outside your comfort zone."

—Robert Allen

So you've come to the end of this book. Hopefully you're thinking, "There are some good ideas in here, I should put them to use." But for some of you, your next thought is something like, "But even if I don't, I'm doing okay — well above average, actually."

That's fine — as long as you don't desire to be highly successful. And maybe you don't. But if you do want to be highly successful, you can't get there by being satisfied.

Highly successful people are never satisfied. They are happy, but never satisfied. They want to reach another, loftier goal. They want to grow. They want to do more, see more, touch more lives.

"Show me a man who is satisfied and I'll show you a failure."

—Thomas Edison

Rarely do I meet a salesperson who will tell me that his goal is to become one of the greatest in his profession. Most tell me they want to be good, or maybe very good. Why not great? What holds us back from achieving that type of success? Only ourselves.

Lance Armstrong is quite possibly one of the most driven and successful athletes of all time. He overcame incredible odds to survive cancer, and then went on to win the Tour de France multiple times. He could have stopped after this first victory and still gone down in history as one of the best sports achievers ever. He could have exalted in the triumph as the pinnacle of his career and simply retired on top. His odds of repeating a win were very slim. Why take the risk of trying again? He risked possibly losing, injuring himself and never competing again, and tarnishing that one shining moment of victory with the lasting memory of a defeat. Armstrong took this challenge not once, but an additional six times! Why? *Because successful people are never satisfied.*

Don't sell yourself short. You can hit a higher level regardless of where you are or how much you have succeeded thus far. What is the most money you think you can make this year — got a sales number in mind? Good. Now double that! Make that your annual sales goal to achieve within the next two years. If you focus on that goal with all of your drive and determination, regardless of the odds against you, you can achieve it.

But you've got to *conceive* it and *believe* it to *achieve* it. You've got to conjure up what your picture of success looks like and then accept it as your truth. And then you've got to go outside your comfort zone to attain it.

Don't Be "in the Zone" — Break Out of It!

*"Men are not prisoners of fate,
but only prisoners of their own minds."*

—Franklin D. Roosevelt

Do you know how zoos keep elephants from escaping? When an elephant is a baby, a trainer attaches a rope to a post in the ground and ties the other end around the baby elephant's leg. The rope is strong enough to hold when the baby tugs on it, so the elephant learns it can't break the rope. It's trained to stay in the area defined by the length of rope. When the elephant grows up, it easily has the strength to break the rope, but it doesn't even try.

Are you so trained to stay within your comfort zone that you won't even try to break out? We all have imaginary tethers, woven from the can'ts and don'ts and limiting beliefs we have collected throughout our lives, often since childhood. But you, like the elephant, can just yank them out of the ground and head on down the road.

When you move outside of your comfort zone, initially your mind will send you all sorts of warning signals, like tension and physical discomfort. Your mind wants to keep you in your standard operating zone. Don't worry, you'll get over it. Remember the first time you rode a bike? Kissed someone? Moved away from home? Went to a job interview? Gave a speech? After you do new things just once, the discomfort drops considerably. Eventually, the more you carry out the new behavior, your discomfort dissipates entirely.

NINE WAYS TO GET GROWING!

If you want to grow your business and grow your wealth, you must grow yourself. When you grow personally you have more to share with others, so you'll be of more value. In turn, they will be willing to pay you more. When you grow personally, you have more skills to rely on in order to reach your goals.

So, how will you grow? Need some ideas? Here, in no particular order, are some ways you can grow and, in doing so, speed your journey to success:

Get Ready for What You Want

Think about what you ultimately want to achieve, what you want to be doing. Will it require additional education? Specific skills? Special materials or tools? Prepare for it now, so when opportunity knocks you'll be ready to take advantage.

Develop New Habits

Ninety percent of our behavior is habitual. But as the saying goes, insanity is doing the same thing over and over and expecting different results (we want to get in shape, but we always hit the snooze button). Develop a new *good* habit every quarter — getting up earlier, working out every day, clearing your e-mails weekly — and chances are, if you stick with it, it'll stay with you for life.

The only difference between a rut and a grave is the depth.

—UNKNOWN

Improve Your Basic Skills

Take courses to improve your writing, speaking and listening skills. A great place to start is by joining Toastmasters International. You'll learn to think on your feet, improve your self-esteem and assertiveness, and become a better communicator (all great networking skills!).

Put It in Writing

Writer Anne Lamott says if you don't capture a good idea, it's just floating out there for someone else to catch. Your good ideas can come in the shower, in the middle of the night, in the car. Keep pen and paper (index cards work great) in every room of the house and on you at all times.

Watch Less TV

One hour less a day gives you 365 hours a year. That's the equivalent of nine 40-hour work weeks! Use that two months of additional time a year to focus on an area of improvement, learning or anything that's productive. Maybe it's learning a new language, sport or musical instrument. Perhaps it's spending quality time with your family, exercising, learning yoga or meditation, making more sales calls, going back to school, or reading.

Read!!!

The easiest and single best thing you can do for an hour a day is read (or listen to audio tapes). Keep it to nonfiction and you can't help but expand your knowledge — biographies, psychology, sales, philosophy, religion, history, science, health or personal improvement. Take a course in speed-reading and you'll be able to read even more books!

(Try a PhotoReading course, www.learningstrategies.com.)

The large library you will amass also serves as a way to give value to your clients. You can share your knowledge, give a great book as a gift, recommend helpful titles, or even loan out books and tapes (go to www.knockknock.biz for your own library kit).

Get Coached

Go to success and personal development training, seminars, conferences and retreats. Find a mentor — ask someone who excels in sales to share their secrets. Find someone to be your coach, to hold you accountable to your goals and provide continual reinforcement. Consider hiring a personal coach or a business coach (you can find them on the Internet).

Nurture a Passion

Take a course or lessons in something that interests you. You'll grow, it'll make you more interesting, and it'll give you another shared interest with others.

Brian, an insurance agent, always regretted that he didn't learn an instrument when he was young. At the age of 37 he decided to take guitar lessons. Learning to read music and play an instrument as an adult was not easy. The experience taught him humility, patience and persistence. At first the music he made was rather unpleasant. But today he can play the songs he enjoys and entertains himself and others.

Share a Passion

Brian enjoyed learning to play the guitar so much that he encouraged three of his friends (two of whom were also clients) to learn to play various instruments. Then he convinced his guitar teacher to lead them in a rock band (which they named, appropriately, Midlife Crisis). For his fortieth birthday Brian rented a 1,500-seat theater and the band played a benefit concert for a local performing arts high school. The sold-out crowd of family, friends and clients shared in his "rock and roll fantasy" and helped a worthy cause. (Now clients often ask the band to play benefit concerts for the charities they are involved in.)

These are just a few ways to move beyond your comfort zone and in doing so grow your circle of influence and, ultimately, your sales.

The world really is your oyster. Open it wide and enjoy!

"Every morning you wake up with a clean slate. You can make your business, as well as your life, anything you choose it to be."

—MARK SANBORN

Suggested Reading

On Selling:

Collaborative Selling: How to Gain the Competitive Advantage in Sales, by Tony Alessandra

Get More Referrals Now!, by Bill Cates

Effort-Less Marketing for Financial Advisors, by Steve Moeller

Love Is the Killer App: How to Win Business and Influence Friends, by Tim Sanders

Questions Great Financial Advisors Ask, by Alan Parisse and David Richman

Secrets of Question-Based Selling: How the Most Powerful Tool in Business Can Double Your Sales Results, by Thomas A. Freese

SuperNetworking For Sales Pros: Access The Right People, Strengthen Client Relationships, And Double Your Sales, by Michael Salmon

The Little Red Book of Selling: The 12.5 Principles of Sales Greatness, by Jeffrey Gitomer

On Work and Attitude:

Getting Things Done: The Art of Stress-Free Productivity, by David Allen

The Fred Factor: How Passion in Your Work and Life Can Turn the Ordinary into the Extraordinary, by Mark Sanborn

How Full is Your Bucket? Positive Strategies for Work and Life, by Tom Rath and Donald O. Clifton

On Success:

The 7 Habits of Highly Effective People: Powerful Lessons in Personal Change, by Stephen R. Covey

The Monk Who Sold His Ferrari: A Fable About Fulfilling Your Dreams and Reaching Your Destiny, by Robin S. Sharma

The Success Principles: How to Get from Where Your Are to Where You Want to Be, by Jack Canfield with Janet Switzer

True Success: A New Philosophy of Excellence, by Tom Morris

About the Author

As chief sales strategist for Federated Investors, Tony Fadool addresses financial intermediaries on a wide variety of investment topics and on how they can build their businesses. He has been a featured speaker at numerous seminars for the American Banking Association, Bank Securities Association and Securities Industry Association. In addition, he presents several public seminars on investing each year.

Combining humor and personal anecdotes, Tony draws on his nearly 40 years of experience in the securities industry as a broker, wholesaler and sales manager. He presents a unique perspective for intermediaries and investors as to how they can build wealth, regardless of what the market is doing.

Before becoming chief sales strategist at Federated Investors, Tony was national sales manager with the company for 10 years. Prior to that, he spent more than 10 years with Merrill Lynch and eight years as president of a bank-owned brokerage firm, Signet Investment Services. He holds a B.S. in business administration and management from Virginia Commonwealth University and has completed graduate courses in management at the University of Michigan.

You can reach Tony at tfadool@federatedinv.com.